Lucius Fairchild

Other Badger Biographies

Lucius Fairchild

CIVIL WAR HERO

Stuart Stotts

Wisconsin Historical Society Press

Published by the Wisconsin Historical Society Press
Publishers since 1855

© 2010 by the State Historical Society of Wisconsin

For permission to reuse material from *Lucius Fairchild: Civil War Hero* [978-0-87020-460-9], please access www.copyright.com or contact the Copyright Clearance Center, Inc. (CCC), 222 Rosewood Drive, Danvers, MA 01923, 978-750-8400. CCC is a not-for-profit organization that provides licenses and registration for a variety of users.

wisconsin history.org

Photographs identified with WHi are from the Society's collections; address requests to reproduce these photos to the Visual Materials Archivist at Wisconsin Historical Society, 816 State Street, Madison, WI 53706.

Printed in the United States of America
Designed by Jill Bremigan

14 13 12 11 10   1 2 3 4 5

Library of Congress Cataloging-in-Publication Data
Stotts, Stuart, 1957-
    Lucius Fairchild : Civil War hero / Stuart Stotts. — 1st ed.
        p. cm. — (Badger biographies)
    Includes index.
    ISBN 978-0-87020-460-9 (pbk. : alk. paper) 1. Fairchild, Lucius, 1831-1896—Juvenile literature.
2. Generals—United States—Biography—Juvenile literature. 3. United States—History—Civil War, 1861-1865—Biography—Juvenile literature. 4. Wisconsin—History—Civil War, 1861-1865—Biography—Juvenile literature. 5. United States. Army. Iron Brigade (1861-1865)—Biography—Juvenile literature. 6. Gettysburg, Battle of, Gettysburg, Pa., 1863—Juvenile literature. 7. Governors—Wisconsin—Biography—Juvenile literature. 8. Soldiers—Wisconsin—Biography—Juvenile literature. I. Title.
    E467.1.F225S76 2010
    355.0092—dc22
    [B]

                              2010013945

Front cover: WHi Image ID 1884. Back cover: WHi Image ID 6601.

∞ The paper used in this publication meets the minimum requirements of the American National Standard for Information Sciences—Permanence of Paper for Printed Library Materials, ANSI Z39.48-1992.

Publication was made possible, in part, by a gift in memory of our mother and grandmother, Mary Lee Meyer and Frances Fairchild Gary— George L. N. Meyer Family Foundation. Additional funding was provided by a grant from the Alice E. Smith fellowship fund.

Contents

1

What Makes a Hero?

Wars create heroes. They always have. Through some mixture of courage, cleverness, strength, and just plain luck, a few soldiers who return from the horrors of war shine with the glow of **heroism**.

People admire bravery. They admire **sacrifices** others make. They admire leaders. Maybe people wish they had such qualities themselves. Maybe heroes actually bring out heroic qualities in people around them. Or maybe everyone just loves a good heroic story.

Heroes seem larger than life. Their service or their sacrifice lifts them above others. This position gives them power and influence to make a difference in the world, even as it changes who they are.

---

heroism (**her** oh iz uhm): bravery **sacrifice** (**sak** ruh fls): the act of giving up one thing for another thing

Lucius Fairchild was born in 1831 in the state of Ohio. At that time, the United States was a country that was rapidly **expanding**. **Immigrants** from Europe and people from the South and East were looking for new opportunities in the

WHI IMAGE ID 6601

This is Lucius in 1865, 2 years after he lost his arm at the battle of Gettysburg.

unsettled lands north of the Ohio River and west of the Mississippi River.

The United States was also a country divided into free states and slave states. Western expansion and questions about slavery were both **issues** that shaped Lucius Fairchild's life. His choices defined the man who became first a war hero and then a

expanding: growing larger **immigrant** (**im** uh gruhnt): a person from one country who moves to settle permanently in another **issue**: a point to be debated

2

governor. Though Lucius went West in search of gold, joined the army in search of **glory** in the bloodiest war in the history of the United States, and came home in search of public office, he will always be known best for his sacrifice in war. We remember him as the governor with the empty sleeve.

This is his story.

governor: the person elected as the head of the state to represent all of the people of the state
glory: great praise and honor

2

Young Lucius

✦

Lucius Fairchild was born on December 27, 1831, in Portage County, Ohio, near Cleveland. His mother, Sally, was from Massachusetts, and his father, Jarius, came from New York. Lucius had an older sister, Sarah; an older brother, Cassius; and a younger brother, Charles.

Lucius was 15 when his family moved to Madison, Wisconsin, from Ohio in 1846.

Jarius Fairchild did many different kinds of work during his life. He worked in a **tannery**. He owned a store. He worked as an **auction agent** and as a **customs official**. He used the money he made at his jobs to start new businesses.

Despite his many business failures, Lucius's father Jarius became Madison's first mayor in 1856.

Still, as hard as he tried, Jarius was not very successful as a businessman. He went **bankrupt** several times. And once, he even ended up in prison for owing money! He was so busy with his work that he had very little time for his children. Lucius wanted his father's attention and didn't understand why Jarius was gone so often. Lucius needed someone to provide advice and affection, but his father rarely offered him either. As a result, Lucius had a troubled childhood.

---

tannery: a place where leather is made from animal hides   **auction agent**: person in charge of a public sale, where items are sold to the person offering the most money for them   **customs official**: a person who collects taxes, paid to the government, on items brought in from foreign countries   **bankrupt**: without enough money to pay what a person owes

Lucius did not like school, and he didn't go very often. He preferred playing outside, exploring the streets of Cleveland, and going to dances and on sleigh rides. His mother wasn't able to control him, and his father was gone too often and too long to make a difference.

Jarius Fairchild tried his hand at many different businesses and was often in debt. This record is for a $5,000 loan.

Lucius was kicked out of one school for fighting. He was **expelled** from another for putting a cow in the church pulpit one Sunday.

Still, Lucius seems to have been a likable child. Even with his gift for mischief, he often got his own way. He was curious and playful, and other children often followed his lead in games and activities.

expelled: forced to leave

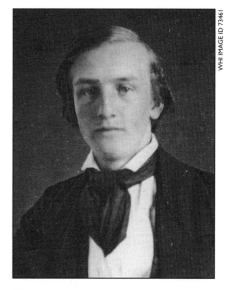

WHI IMAGE ID 73461

In 1846, when Lucius was 15, his family moved to Madison, Wisconsin. His father wanted a fresh start in business. He also hoped that Lucius might improve his education in a new location.

Jarius started a store, and Lucius went to a school near Milwaukee. Three months later, Lucius quit school. It was Lucius's last **formal** education.

This is a picture of young Lucius, before he left for his adventures out west.

He returned to Madison to work in his father's store.

Even though Lucius wasn't a big reader, one book did change his life. In 1848, he read a book called ***Commerce** of the Prairies*. It included descriptions of the West such as, "numerous spring fed **rills** and gurgling **rivulets** . . . in every direction . . . swarms of trout and perch carelessly playing . . . soil dark and mellow, and . . . rich **vegetation**," which excited Lucius's imagination. The idea of open spaces and new business opportunities appealed to Lucius's adventurous side.

formal: organized with a set of rules   **commerce:** the buying and selling of goods in large amounts
rill: a brook   **rivulet:** a very small stream   **vegetation** (vej uh **tay** shuhn): plant life such as trees and grasses

The Expanding West

Throughout the early 1800s, the United States continued to expand westward. Immigrants from Europe would have had little opportunity to own land in their native countries. Some settlers from the eastern states also wanted to own their own land.

To meet the needs of these settlers, the U.S. government needed land for the nation to grow—even if this meant Native American Indians lost their homelands. The country gained **territory** from wars, **treaties** with Indian nations, and **purchases**.

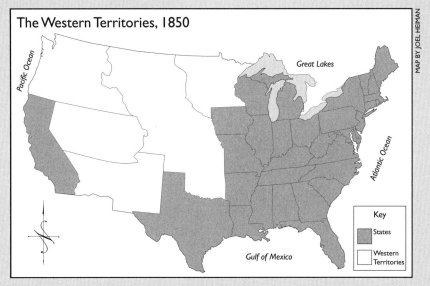

The Western Territories, 1850

Pacific Ocean

Great Lakes

Atlantic Ocean

MAP BY JOEL HEIMAN

Key

States

Western Territories

Gulf of Mexico

In 1850, most the lands west of the Mississippi River were territories—not yet states. Few people lived there.

territory (**ter** uh tor ree): land   **treaty**: an official written document between 2 nations
purchase: something that is bought.

For example, in 1848, as a result of the Mexican American War, Mexico had to give the United States parts of what are now Texas, Colorado, Arizona, New Mexico, and Wyoming as well as all of California. Similarly, in the 1830s in Wisconsin, the U.S. government used the Black Hawk War as an opportunity to get land for settlers, in this case, from treaties with Indian nations.

Hundreds of thousands of settlers traveled west for land and for a new start in life.

In 1848, gold was discovered in California. Lucius spent hours talking with his friends about what became known as the gold rush. That's when thousands of young men such as Lucius headed to California. Soon, 2 of Lucius's friends decided to join him. They all planned to set out to California to make their **fortune**.

Each young man put up a share of money to buy a wagon, some oxen, and **provisions**. Jarius put up Lucius's share and gave him some money for emergencies.

---

fortune: a great deal of money or property   **provision** (pruh **vizh** uhn): a supply of food

9

Madison was a small village when Lucius was a young man, as you can see in this sketch from 1852. Can you find the capitol?

Before he left, Lucius looked back at Madison from a spot on a hill north of the town. This hill later became the center of the University of Wisconsin. Years later, he wrote a letter to his brother about that moment. He said, "Never did a boy feel worse than I did, when I reached the College hill and turned around to take a last long look on the little village that held all that I held dear on earth. . . . I felt when out of sight that I was alone in the world, and **endeavored** to **nerve** myself to the task and be a man."

endeavored (en **dev** urd): tried   **nerve**: to work up the courage for

Lucius rode away from Madison on a black pony. He joined the wagons that were headed west, but he felt homesick for a few hours. Soon, though, the thrill of adventure overcame his doubts. As Lucius himself might have put it, he had "nerved" himself to the task, and he was now ready for his journey west.

3

Gold Rush Fever

Thousands of men and women headed to California in 1849, lured by the promise of gold. "Gold rush fever" brought them, although few of them ever found much in the way of **nuggets**. **Panning** requires skill, a good share of luck, and plenty of hard work.

Lucius wanted adventure and was ready to work hard. He wanted to prove himself, far away from his family's influence. But he also wanted to make money. He said he wanted to make his "pile," and he was determined to come home a rich man.

Lucius was affected by his **upbringing**. He felt **insecure** because of his father's frequent business failures. Lucius thought that if he could become rich, he would escape his constant fear of not having enough money. These fears had upset his childhood.

nugget: a small, rough piece of valuable metal   **panning**: washing gravel or sand in a pan, so the gold becomes separate
upbringing: the care and training given to children when they are growing up   **insecure**: not confident of oneself

The Gold Rush

News of the 1848 discovery of gold in California spread throughout the United States and the world. More than 300,000 men, women, and children traveled to California to seek their fortune. That's why California came to be known as the "Golden State."

These early gold seekers were called "forty-niners" because many headed for California in 1849. They traveled by sailing ship and by covered wagon. They faced many difficulties on the long journey west. Once they arrived, they found that living conditions were harsh, and even simple goods and necessities were very expensive.

At first, the **prospectors** panned gold from streams and rivers. Later they developed better methods to recover the gold by blasting hills apart with powerful jets of water. However, mining damaged the **environment** by **polluting** streams and destroying forest **habitats**. As a result, many Native people were pushed out of their homelands, and many died from starvation and disease.

Few forty-niners actually found millions of dollars worth of gold. Few prospectors grew as wealthy as they had hoped. By the mid-1850s, the Gold Rush ended, and most miners returned home with little more than when they started. There was only so much gold in the hills to find. Disappointment, not wealth, was the theme of most stories among the forty-niners.

---

prospector: someone who explores an area looking for valuable resources   **environment** (en **vl** ruhn muhnt): the natural world of land, sea, and air in which people, animals, and plants live   **polluting** (puh **loot** ing): dirtying or destroying the natural environment   **habitat**: the place or environment where a plant or animal naturally or normally lives

13

Lucius's trip was filled with adventures. Fortunately, he wrote many letters that described his travels.

In one letter to his mother, Lucius wrote, "A man from Independence [Missouri] who went to California last fall writes home that he is making with his family $500 to $1,000 per day. There may be a chance for [me] to fill my pockets. If so, mother, you shall have half."

First, Lucius took a boat south, down the Mississippi River. He wrote, "I had a first rate trip down, only we were on a miserable poor boat and the captain cheated me out of $3.35 . . . it could not be helped without trouble, so we gave it to him. Still, experience bought is better than experience taught."

Lucius and his traveling friends took 6 weeks just to get to the starting point of the **wagon train**, in Council Bluffs, Iowa. They had fought mud and rain and had seen their wagon tip over into the mud twice before their westward journey had even truly begun!

wagon train: many wagons traveling together as a group

Early in May, Lucius's party joined a wagon train and set out for California. Every day there was the same **routine**. Lucius described it in a letter.

> We are waked at 1/2 past 3 in the morning to untie the cattle to feed, then make a fire and cook breakfast as soon as possible. We have fried meat, coffee and bread. As soon as that is over the order is given to bring up the cattle who by this time have filled themselves and laid down. **Yoke up** and start out each one leading in his turn and then going to the last end of the train and work up to the head. Travel until 12 1/2 o'clock and [eat lunch]. Make our dinner of cold pancakes cooked the night before then smoke and start and go on 'til 4 o'clock. Then camp whether we are near water and timber or not ... by the time we get supper out of the way and cooking done for the next day it is time to go and herd the cattle and let them eat until they all lay down then tie them in the

routine (roo **teen**): the regular or usual method for doing things   **yoke up**: attach work animals to a wood frame, so they can pull a wagon or other equipment

ring. By the time this is all done we are tired enough to go directly to bed so that we do not have much time to mend clothes or loaf about reading.

It was hard and slow traveling, but Lucius enjoyed it. He was surprised at how many wagon trains there were. On any given day, he could see hundreds of wagons. With so many wagons, travelers could not be **ambushed** or attacked easily.

Lucius and his friends found that their wagon was too heavy. They had to throw away some **items** that they did not need. For example, they had brought heavy rope and a **block and tackle**, because they thought that they might have to pull and lift their wagon over the Rocky Mountains! They threw these heavy items away when they realized that they could merely follow other wagons through **passes** in the mountains.

They finally reached California, 6 months after they started out from Wisconsin.

ambushed: attacked from a hiding place   **item**: thing or object   **block and tackle**: a device with a heavy weight at one end, a pulley in the middle, and a hook on the other end; it makes the task of lifting heavy objects easier   **pass**: a gap or place of lower elevation

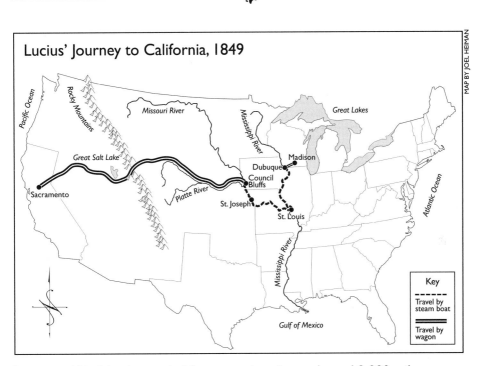

MAP BY JOEL HEIMAN

Lucius' Journey to California, 1849

Pacific Ocean

Rocky Mountains

Missouri River

Great Lakes

Great Salt Lake

Mississippi River

Madison

Dubuque

Council Bluffs

Platte River

Sacramento

St. Joseph

St. Louis

Atlantic Ocean

Mississippi River

Gulf of Mexico

Key

- - - - - Travel by steam boat

═════ Travel by wagon

Lucius and his friends traveled for more than 6 months and 2,000 miles to reach California.

When they arrived in Sacramento, California, Lucius and his friends sold their wagon and oxen. They bought food to last through the winter, and they began to pan for gold.

Life was not easy. Food was expensive. Lucius wrote, "I have not tasted vegetables of any kind or butter since leaving." Tools and clothing were expensive, too. A pair of boots could cost from $30 to $60. In today's money, that would be more than $1,000!

The prospectors lived in rough cabins. They slept on mattresses filled with leaves, although Lucius said, "You cannot imagine the comfort we take with a good house and fireplace, after being **deprived** of them, and sleeping on the ground for over 7 months."

They worked hard all day but often came back empty-handed or with barely enough gold to cover their **expenses**.

In the gold rush, prospectors bought or **staked claims** of land to work a certain part of a stream. The price of these claims rose and fell, depending on how much gold had been found nearby. A successful prospector could pan for gold on his claim or could try to sell the claim to another prospector who wanted to take a chance there.

Lucius described the work. "Each man is **entitled** to 100 feet of the whole creek up and down . . . work enough for two or three years if all of ground paid, but only a small strip does and that is hard to find."

deprived: kept from   **expense**: the money spent on something   **staked claims**: paid money for the chance to find gold in a specific location   **entitled** (en tɪ tuhld): has a claim to

18

Over the next few months, when he did find gold, Lucius used his money to buy new claims. Those purchases almost never paid off, and he had to start over again, panning in the rivers and creeks. Lucius formed partnerships with many different men. He hoped that one of them would lead to a fortune. None of them did.

In one of his letters sent home from California, Lucius wrote: "The longer I stay here the more I want to return."

But Lucius didn't just pan for gold. He helped farm. He waited tables. And he learned to butcher cattle to make a living. His willingness to work hard caught the attention of Elijah Steele. He and Lucius became business partners. Their business wasn't gold, however. It was beef. Lucius and Elijah sold meat to miners, and that's when Lucius finally began to make a good living. In the meat business, Lucius made the "pile" he had not been able to make in panning for gold.

Lucius would even lend money to other prospectors so that they could buy claims and start searching for gold. He said, "My object in paying money to have that hill prospected was to get diggings to keep more men on the river *So I can sell them Beef.*" He learned that there was more money in serving those who looked for gold than in looking for gold himself.

Finally, Lucius had found success. In 1855, after 6 years in California, he sold the beef business to Steele for $10,000 (about $250,000 in today's money). He had made his "pile."

Not only had Lucius made his money, but he also got his first **political** experience. Like his father Jarius, Lucius was a member of the **Democratic Party**. In 1853 he was chosen to be a **delegate** to the state's Democratic **convention**. He started for the convention from Calaveras County in northern California, with his clothes loaded on a mule. The convention was about 100 miles away, near San Francisco.

Lucius traveled through wild country. At one point, his mule fell over a cliff and was carried away in a river far below. Lucius

political (puh **lit** uh kuhl): having to do with the way a city, county, state, or nation governs itself
Democratic Party: one of the 2 main political parties in the United States   **delegate** (**del** uh git): someone who is given power or authority to act for others   **convention**: a large gathering of people from the same political party

kept on walking until he was able to catch a stagecoach. He walked the last part of the journey as well, and arrived at the convention in time to cast a vote for the Democratic candidate.

By this time, Lucius had had enough of California and his gold mining adventures. He took his money and boarded a ship heading south. He crossed Panama by land, because a canal wasn't built there until more than 50 years later. And then he took a second ship north to New York City. From there, he took a train to Madison. He was quite a sight, dressed in mining clothes, with high-heeled top boots, a big **sombrero**, and his money in a belt around his waist. He was only 23

WHI IMAGE ID 73456

The hat Lucius is wearing here is a sombrero, typical of forty-niners.

sombrero (som **brer** oh): a hat whose wide brim helps block the sun

when he returned, but he was changed. Lucius was no longer a mischievous boy; he was a lean, experienced, and wealthy young man.

Lucius later wrote about his time in California: "I think that I owe very much to this part of my life. I was forced to depend on my own energy. Since that period I have always been fond of work, and glad to have plenty of it. . . . We had many ups and downs . . . but this experience was of the greatest **benefit** to me in my life."

benefit: anything that is for the good of someone or something

22

4

Captain Fairchild

When Lucius returned to Madison, much of his hard-earned money went into his father's **investments**. Jarius had invested money in railroads, as well as in coal and ice businesses. But, as usual, he wasn't doing well.

Lucius worked for a railroad for a while, until it went bankrupt. Then his father advised him to go into **politics**. Jarius had been elected the first mayor of Madison, and Lucius's brother Cassius was also very involved in the local Democratic Party. Lucius could see that by being elected to a political office, he could get a regular **salary**. He would also be able to use his influence to help his family's interests.

Lucius began to join community organizations. He became a member of 3 churches. He joined the volunteer fire department. And he joined the Governor's Guard, a local **militia**.

investment: something purchased with the hope that it will generate additional money   **politics**: the way a city, state, or nation governs itself   **salary** (**sal** ur ee): money that you get paid for work that you do
militia (muh **lish** uh): a volunteer army trained to fight only in an emergency

Militias were groups of citizens who learned military skills without actually joining the army. They were, however, ready to fight if they were needed to defend the community.

The Governor's Guard was a unit that was mostly **ceremonial**. They met weekly for military **drills**. During the drills, the guard practiced marching in **formation**, using their rifles, and

WHI IMAGE ID 1872

After returning from California, Lucius volunteered with the Madison Fire Department.

following orders. The men also dressed up in their uniforms for these drills and for dances. Lucius was quickly elected **lieutenant** to the Guard. He was popular and **straightforward** with his men. The men could imagine that Lucius had a certain heroic glow as a returning gold rush **veteran**.

ceremonial (ser uh **moh** nee uhl): taking place for a traditional or formal purpose more than for practical use
drill: lesson on how to do something by doing it over and over again **formation**: a special arrangement of troops and of military equipment **lieutenant** (loo **ten** uhnt): a military rank below captain and above sergeant **straightforward**: honest, direct **veteran**: someone who has lots of experience doing something

Military Ranks

Military ranks establish the order of power. The ranks may be different in different branches of the military, but in the army generals are at the top, and privates are at the bottom. From the top down, the order of military rank in the army is as follows:

1. General	4. Major	7. Sergeant
2. **Colonel**	5. Captain	8. Corporal
3. Lieutenant	6 Lieutenant	9. Private

The higher the rank, the more soldiers the officer commands. For example, a lieutenant is usually in charge of about 50 soldiers.

All of this "joining" led to Lucius's first political office. In 1858, he was elected **clerk** of the Dane County Court. Most of his responsibilities involved collecting **taxes** and **fees**. He did not enjoy the county clerk job much. He described it as "dry business having old musty law discussed." Lucius said it "paid well," though, and soon he had enough money to buy a **dry goods store** with his brother Charles. Lucius agreed to pay many of his father's **debts**. Lucius wrote, "I have a great horror of being 'short' of money. It would take all comfort out of the

colonel (**kur** nuhl)   clerk: someone who works in an office and files records   tax: money paid to the government   fee: money paid for a service that is performed   **dry goods store**: a general store selling a variety of items, such as sugar, tools, and cloth   debt (det): money that is owed to someone

world for me. I shall never be [penniless] if I can help it." He knew that he would have to work hard so as not to repeat his father's **financial** mistakes in his own life.

Lucius was well liked as county clerk. The *Patriot* newspaper said, "Never were the duties of the office more faithfully **discharged** than during Mr. Fairchild's term."

Even so, Lucius lost his bid to be re-elected as county clerk. After losing the election, Lucius began to work as a lawyer. He relied on what he had learned as county clerk. He also watched what was happening **nationally**. Like President Lincoln, Lucius felt that the South could not be allowed to **secede** from the **Union**. The South was full of Democrats who wanted to secede. Lucius left the Democratic Party. He wanted to be prepared to take part in the Civil War that he saw coming.

WHI IMAGE ID 8007

President Lincoln in 1865.

financial (fi **nan** shuhl): having to do with money   **discharged**: carried out; performed   **nationally**: across or throughout a nation   **secede** (si **seed**): to leave or withdraw from a group or an organization, often to form another   **Union**: the group of states that remained loyal to the United States government during the Civil War; the North

Free and Slave States and the Civil War

Throughout much of the first half of the 1800s, people in different regions of the United States argued over the question of slavery. People from the South generally supported slavery, and most Northerners were against it.

When a new state that allowed slavery entered the Union as a slave state, it had to be balanced out by another new state that entered as a free state. For example, Texas entered as a slave state in 1846, while Wisconsin entered as a free state in 1848. Many people in the South were worried that free states—many with larger numbers of people—had more power. These Southerners began to feel that they wanted to secede from the Union and form their own country. That way, slavery would be allowed everywhere in this separate country.

The Democratic Party had been formed in the early 1800s, and most eligible voters in the South were Democrats who favored secession.

In 1854, some antislavery members of the Democratic Party met with others in Ripon, Wisconsin. They formed the Republican Party, which opposed new states becoming slave states.

In 1856, the first Republican candidate, John C. Fremont, ran for president of this party, but he did not win. In 1860, Abraham

Lincoln felt strongly that the Union must not be divided. The South did not support Lincoln, but in 1860 Lincoln won a close race and became the first Republican president.

After Lincoln was elected, more Southerners wanted to secede from the United States. In fact, before Lincoln took office in March 1861, 7 Southern states had already seceded: first, South Carolina, followed by Mississippi, Florida, Alabama, Georgia, Louisiana, and Texas. These states named their new country the **Confederate** States of America. The people there became known as Confederates or **rebels**.

In 1854, the Republican Party was started in this small schoolhouse located in Ripon, Wisconsin.

Confederate (kuhn **fed** ur it): relating to the 11 Southern states that fought the Northern states in the American Civil War **rebel**: In the Civil War, someone on the side of the Confederates

The Civil War began on April 12, 1861, soon after Abraham Lincoln was elected president. Confederate troops attacked Fort Sumter, a Union fort off the coast of South Carolina. Four more Southern states soon joined the Confederacy: Arkansas, North Carolina, Virginia, and Tennessee, for a total of 11 states.

The Confederate soldiers wore uniforms of grey. The remaining Northern states became known as the Union. Union states were fighting for the country to stay together, or united. Their uniforms were blue. The Confederates were successful in the beginning of the war, but by 1865, they had **surrendered** to the Union, and the United States became one country again. In this bloody, 4-year war, more than 600,000 Americans died as a result of fighting or disease.

When war broke out in 1861, President Lincoln called for volunteers, and Wisconsin governor Alexander Randall answered. Lucius Fairchild was quick to offer himself.

surrendered (suh **ren** durd): given up

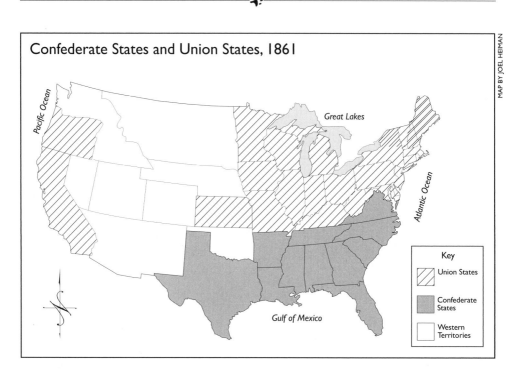

Confederate States and Union States, 1861

Pacific Ocean

Great Lakes

Atlantic Ocean

Gulf of Mexico

Key

Union States

Confederate States

Western Territories

MAP BY JOEL HEIMAN

The state created Camp Randall—a training ground in Madison for soldiers. About 70,000 soldiers would train there for the war. That ground is where the University of Wisconsin's football stadium now stands.

Like many young men, Lucius was ready to fight as soon as the war began. He said, "I am going to take a hand in it, if I can do in any **station** above a private. . . . I don't know of anybody who can take a **clatter** at that kind of fun any more **conveniently** than [I can]."

station: position **clatter**: an attempt or a try **conveniently** (kuhn **vee** nyuhnt lee): easily

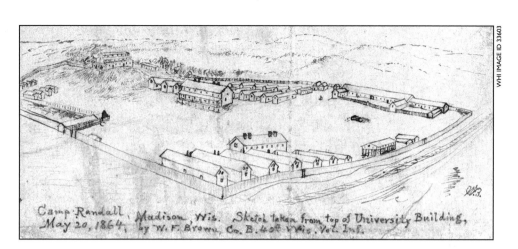

This is a sketch of Camp Randall in Madison. The long narrow buildings housed soldiers. Can you see the date of the sketch?

Like most Americans, Lucius could not imagine the horrible nature of the battle ahead for the nation. But his desire for adventure and his belief in the **unity** of the United States led him forward.

By this time, the members of the Governor's Guard had elected Lucius captain, and the governor soon **confirmed** this honor. However, when Governor Randall offered him the higher rank of lieutenant colonel, Lucius refused. "I do not feel **competent** to discharge the duties," he said. Lucius was naturally **modest**.

unity (yoo ni tee): being in agreement   **confirmed**: approved of   **competent (kom** puh tuhnt): capable
modest: not thinking too highly of oneself

He was also realistic. He understood his **limitations**. Lucius did not want responsibilities for which he was not prepared. He did not want to put his men in dangers he could not handle as their leader.

Many men who joined the military hoped to climb up the ranks quickly, for greater honor and greater pay. It was very unusual for someone to turn down a higher rank. This action added to Lucius's **reputation** as a fair and honest man.

Captain Lucius Fairchild led his men in military drills. He also spent part of his days walking the streets of Madison **recruiting** new men to join the army. The Governor's Guard became part of the First Wisconsin **Regiment**. The regiment signed up for 3 months of duty.

Wisconsin eventually sent more than 80,000 soldiers of all ranks to the Civil War. More than 12,000 of them died.

limitation: where something ends   **reputation** (rep yoo **tay** shuhn): the opinion that people have about someone or something   **recruiting** (re **kroo** ting): getting people to join a group, especially the military **regiment** (**rej** uh muhnt): part of the army (500 to 1,000 soldiers) under the command of a colonel

How Soldiers Are Organized

Soldiers are organized into groups of different sizes. Generally, a squad is the smallest, and an army is the largest. The order of size is different in different countries and different branches of the military, but in the Civil War, the order was as follows:

1. Army: 2 or more **corps**
2. Corps: 3 divisions
3. Division: 3 or 4 **brigades**
4. Brigade: 4 or 5 regiments
5. Regiment: 500 to 1,000 soldiers
6. **Battalion** : 100 to 500 soldiers
7. Company: 50 to 100 soldiers
8. Platoon: 25 to 50 soldiers
9. Section: 12 to 25 soldiers
10. Squad: 12 or fewer soldiers

corps: (cor)   **brigade**: (bri **gayd**)   **battalion**: (buh **tal** yuhn)

5

The Battle of Brawner's Farm

Late in April of 1861, Lucius and his men left Madison. They spent a month in Milwaukee, training and waiting. Lucius felt ready for war. "I'd give all my pay to be able to take a hand in the fight just once this week," he wrote. He still had the spirit of adventure that had led him to the gold rush years earlier. He was hungry for the excitement he thought war would offer him and his men.

By June, the First Wisconsin had shipped out by train to Pennsylvania and then on to Maryland. In July his unit had a small **encounter** with Confederate forces in northern Virginia. But mostly they marched and did not see action.

Lucius and his men had signed up for only 3 months. By August, they were free to return home. Lucius tried to convince his men to stay, but most men had had enough of army life.

encounter: an unexpected meeting or conflict

Unlike the First Wisconsin, the Second Wisconsin Regiment had many problems. Some of the commanders were poor leaders. Some were afraid of fighting. The men were **undisciplined** because they had been serving under poor leaders.

WISCONSIN VETERANS MUSEUM

Soldiers in the Second Wisconsin Regiment carried this flag into battle.

Governor Randall wanted Wisconsin's soldiers to be a force he could be proud of. He remembered that Lucius had refused the governor's earlier offer of a higher rank. Governor Randall again appointed Lucius to be a lieutenant colonel in the army, and this time Lucius accepted. The governor moved Lucius from the First to the Second Wisconsin Regiment. He hoped that Lucius would be the kind of leader who could improve that regiment.

undisciplined (un **dis** uh plind): untrained or out of control

Lucius went back to Madison briefly. Friends and citizens celebrated his new rank. When Lucius returned to army life, he found himself under the command of 2 colonels. Soldiers disliked these colonels for their laziness and their drunkenness. Lucius began to drill the soldiers, and he gained their admiration. He did not place himself above his men. That is, he did everything himself that he ordered them to do, whether that meant marching or exercising or training with weapons. Lucius's willingness to share their experiences made him a popular leader.

For nearly a year, Lucius and the Second Wisconsin trained as they waited for an assignment to fight. The idea of "hurry up and wait" is common in war, and it was true for Lucius and his men at the time.

One Wisconsin soldier described life in training. "A military life in camp is the most **monotonous** in the world. It is the same routine over and over every day."

The men passed their time playing card games, playing chess and checkers, and talking about politics. Soldiers also tired of

monotonous (muh **not** un nuhs): boring because of sameness the endless marching and drilling. They felt eager and ready to fight.

Jarius Fairchild died during 1862, and Lucius's mother visited Lucius. Lucius attended a few military dances and events. He also occasionally went to Washington for visits, but mostly, he and his men waited in Camp Advance, Virginia, near Washington, D.C.

In August of 1862, Lucius was finally part of a real battle. The Second Wisconsin was under the command of General John Pope. They were trying to trap Confederate general Stonewall Jackson near Gainesville, Virginia. Instead, Pope's forces themselves marched into an ambush, in what would later become known as the battle of Brawner's Farm.

Lucius was lying ill at the time. He heard the shooting, leapt up, and rushed into battle. His men cheered as he reached the front lines. They fought fiercely. Lucius's horse was shot out from under him, but his men held their ground amid many **casualties**. The number of casualties was high, because it also included soldiers who were simply labeled "missing."

casualty (**kazh** oo uhl tee): someone who has been wounded, killed, or injured in a battle

Civil War battles were often confusing. Amid the smoke and bullets, it was hard to know what was happening. **Communication** depended on messengers and reports. At one point in this battle, Lucius ran to find Colonel Robinson, who commanded the Seventh Wisconsin Regiment. Lucius said, "For God's sake, Colonel, deliver your fire up to the left. We are all cut to pieces, and the enemy are advancing on us."

Robinson gave the order. A Seventh Wisconsin soldier remembered, "Company after company [of Wisconsin soldiers] came . . . along the foot of the slope, and poured in their [rifle] fire . . . right into the enemy's lines . . . and they broke and fell back. . . . Who does not remember the cheer we gave?"

The fighting continued. Another soldier recalled a scene from the battle: "I could distinctly see Lieutenant Colonel Fairchild, of the 2nd Wisconsin . . . working among and cheering up [his] men. . . . Men who were shot were streaming back from along the whole line . . . our regiment was suffering more than it had been . . . in the history of war,

communication (kuh myoo nuh **kay** shun): giving and receiving information

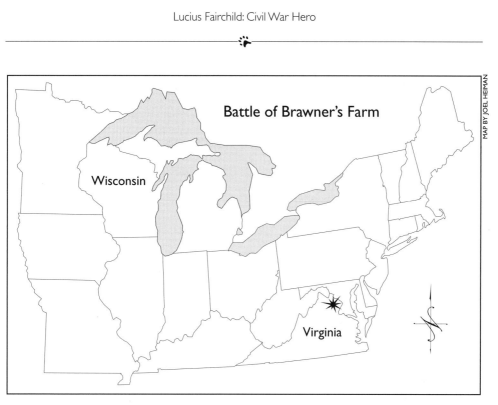

Lucius's men suffered heavy casualties at the battle of Brawner's Farm.

it is doubtful whether there was ever more stubborn courage than was displayed by the 2nd and 7th Wisconsin ... on this field of battle."

Another soldier remembered seeing Lucius. "The Lieutenant Colonel Fairchild was under the hottest fire but escaped unhurt." Lucius was lucky. Many other officers died that day.

The Second, Sixth, and Seventh Wisconsin as well as the Nineteenth Indiana held off the Confederate forces so that the rest of General Pope's soldiers could **retreat**. That night, Lucius gathered his men. He was shaken to see so few. "Where is the regiment, have they scattered?" he asked. Someone replied, "Colonel, this is all that is left of the 2nd, the rest lay on the field." With tears in his eyes, Lucius replied, "Thank God they are worthy of their name." Lucius **grieved** the loss of his men, but he was proud of their courage and honor.

The Second Wisconsin Regiment had fought bravely, but their losses were heavy. By the time they reached camp, nearly 300 out of 500 men were killed, wounded, or missing. Still, after this battle, they gained a reputation for their strength and courage. They were part of the larger unit that became known as the Iron Brigade.

retreat: move back   **grieved**: felt sad for

The Iron Brigade

The Iron Brigade earned its name while under the command of General John Gibbon. The Iron Brigade consisted of about 2,100 soldiers, drawn from 5 regiments: 3 Wisconsin regiments, including Lucius's Second Regiment; one regiment from Indiana; and one from Michigan.

After the battle of Brawner's Farm, General Gibbon's soldiers' reputation for courage and skill grew. At the battle of South Mountain, a month later, Union general George McClellan watched from above as these regiments fought hard against the Confederates. "What troops are those?" he asked General Joseph Hooker. Hooker replied, "General Gibbon's brigade of **western** men." "They must be made of iron," said McClellan. General McClellan added that they must be "the best troops in the world."

These soldiers, wearing tall black hats, fought in the Iron Brigade.

western: of or from the west. Iron Brigade troops came from Wisconsin, Indiana, and Michigan—which were then considered western states

41

The name "iron" stuck and became a source of great pride for the soldiers. They were also known as the "Black Hat Brigade," for their black hats, which were different from the blue hats usually worn by Union troops.

During the Civil War, the Iron Brigade fought in many of the important battles, including Bull Run, Fredericksburg, Antietam, and Gettysburg. By the end of the war, the brigade had suffered more casualties than any other.

So many soldiers had been lost in the Second and the Seventh Wisconsin Regiments that General John Gibbon, who commanded the Iron Brigade, combined the 2 temporarily. He put them under the command of Lucius Fairchild, who was the highest-ranking officer unhurt that day.

Lucius was promoted to colonel for his leadership at the battle of Brawner's Farm. His men were soon on the march again.

Robert E. Lee was the general in charge of the entire Confederate army. He had been very successful. A few days after Brawner's Farm, Lucius and his soldiers fought Lee's army at the second battle of Bull Run.

Lucius waited with his men as the Confederates advanced. When General Gibbon gave the order, the rifles and cannons began to fire. One Wisconsin soldier wrote, "[The blasts] tore great bloody gaps in the Rebel lines and piled the dead and **mangled** in rows like hay raked in a hayfield. . . . The bullets came over our heads like a shower of hailstones. . . . It was a terrible **slaughter**."

This is General Robert E. Lee, who commanded Confederate forces at the second battle of Bull Run.

Over the next month, Lucius and his men fought General Lee at South Mountain and, soon after that, at Antietam Creek. By the end of these battles, out of the 150 who had survived Brawner's Farm, only 15 were still present for duty!

mangled: badly cut or torn   **slaughter**: killing of many people

43

During the Civil War, the government had a **draft**, also known as "conscription." The army told young men that they needed to join and fight. However, men could escape the army by paying for a substitute to take their place. This practice was common and allowed many people to avoid serving in the army. It was obviously unfair and sparked the phrase "rich man's war, but poor man's fight."

Lucius returned to Wisconsin to recruit more soldiers. He discovered that he now had a reputation and a nickname of "the **Gallant** Colonel."

This is a recruiting poster from the Civil War.

draft: the selection of people for a special purpose, especially for serving in the army   **gallant** (gal uhnt): brave

Madison friends asked his opinions on the war. He replied that it had to continue until the North had achieved total victory.

Lucius was very upset to have lost so many of his men. He blamed the war and the Confederate army. Lucius had come to hate everything Southern. He told his sister, "I hope never to be ordered to take a prisoner—I'd rather a dead rebel [Confederate] than a live one and if I ever have the chance, I'll have nothing but dead ones."

Such strong language made Lucius a very memorable figure. He disagreed with the Democratic Party's views on the conflict. His support for the war was total. It was, he wrote, "almost past belief" that anyone would oppose the war and the government.

6

"Thank God I Still Have One [Arm]"

———————— 🐾 ————————

Lucius recruited still more soldiers and trained them. By the end of 1862, he had returned to Virginia. That winter his regiment fought in small battles known as **skirmishes**. Through it all, Lucius continued to demonstrate bravery and strong leadership.

In late June of 1863, the Second Wisconsin marched toward Gettysburg, Pennsylvania. Confederate general Robert E. Lee's forces were **invading** the North. The Union army meant to stop them.

Gettysburg was a small town, and the battle took place in the fields and woods nearby. The Union army was under the command of General George Meade. At this point in the war, General Lee seemed to be **invincible**. His rebel soldiers kept beating the armies of the North. Both Confederate and

skirmish: a small battle   **invading**: entering by force   **invincible** (in **vin** suh buhl): not able to be defeated

Battle of Gettysburg

Wisconsin

Pennsylvania

The Battle of Gettysburg was fought in the woods and fields near Gettysburg, Pennsylvania.

Union troops realized that the future direction of the war was at stake.

As they marched nearby, Lucius's regiment heard the sound of guns and headed toward the battlefield. They marched over a rise at **Willoughby Run** and were immediately met with **volley** after volley of Confederate rifle fire. Almost a third of his 273 men were killed in those **initial** volleys. Lucius was hit with

Willoughby Run (wil uh bee ruhn)   **volley**: a shower of bullets   **initial** (i **nish** uhl): first

This is a drawing of an Enfield musket, a gun often used by Confederate soldiers. The **bayonet** below it fits on the front end.

a **musket ball**, which shattered his left arm above the elbow.

Lucius told his men not to take him away. He wanted to stay to lead the fight. Confederate soldiers captured him, but they soon left him behind when they retreated. Union soldiers later found him. They took Lucius into the town of Gettysburg, where he stayed at a private home. The Second Wisconsin's surgeon had to **amputate** Lucius's arm.

WISCONSIN VETERANS MUSEUM

Lucius wore this vest during the Battle of Gettysburg. The tear in the left shoulder of the vest is where the musket ball struck him.

When Lucius awoke from the operation, he looked down and said, "Thank God I still have one [arm] left."

bayonet (bay uh **net**): a blade that can be attached to the front end of a rifle   musket ball: a lead ball, similar to a bullet but larger, that is shot from a gun called a musket   amputate (am pyuh tate): cut off all or part of a finger, arm, or leg because of disease or injury

As the battle continued, Lucius watched from the porch of the house. He shouted encouragement to the soldiers as they ran by, and he wished he could return to the fight.

For 3 days, the battle raged on. At times the smoke from the gunpowder was so dense that it was difficult to see where the enemy was. It was as if a dense fog lay over the field. Bullets flew so thickly through the air that tree trunks were blown to pieces! The moans of wounded and dying men mixed with rifle volleys and cannon fire. Soldiers fought close at hand with swords, bayonets, and knives. After the battle was over, those who had survived told about the horrors they had seen.

In the end, there were more than 45,000 casualties, and more than 8,000 men lost their lives. Six months after the Battle of Gettysburg, President Lincoln went to the **site** of the battle and delivered the most famous speech in American history. The speech lasted only about 2 minutes. It praised the men who had sacrificed their lives fighting to preserve the Union. The speech inspired people of the Union to continue to support the war. And it still inspires Americans as they remember the sacrifices men made to preserve our country.

site: location, place

49

The Gettysburg Address

"Four score and 7 years ago our fathers brought forth on this continent a new nation, **conceived** in Liberty, and **dedicated** to the **proposition** that all men are created equal.

"Now we are engaged in a great civil war, testing whether that nation, or any nation, so conceived and so dedicated, can long **endure**. We are met on a great battlefield of that war. We have come to dedicate a **portion** of that field, as a final resting place for those who here gave their lives that that nation might live. It is altogether fitting and proper that we should do this.

"But, in a larger sense, we can not dedicate—we can not **consecrate**—we can not **hallow**—this ground. The brave men, living and dead, who struggled here, have consecrated it, far above our poor power to add or **detract**. The world will little note, nor long remember what we say here, but it can never forget what they did here. It is for us the living, rather, to be dedicated here to the unfinished work which they who fought here have thus far so nobly advanced. It is rather for us to be here dedicated to the great task remaining before us—that from these honored dead we take increased **devotion** to that cause for which they gave the last full measure of devotion—that we here

---

4 score and 7 years: 87 years; a score is a group of 20   **conceived**: thought of or imagined   **dedicated**: committed   **proposition**: a plan or idea to be considered   **endure**: keep on   **portion (por** shuhn): a part   **consecrate**: to make sacred   **hallow**: to make holy   **detract**: take away from   **devotion**: a strong feeling of loyalty

highly **resolve** that these dead shall not have died **in vain**—that this nation, under God, shall have a new birth of freedom—and that government of the people, by the people, for the people, shall not **perish** from the earth."

> Four score and seven years ago our fathers brought forth, upon this continent, a new nation, conceived in liberty, and dedicated to the proposition that "all men are created equal"

Abraham Lincoln's powerful Gettysburg Address lasted only 2 minutes. It is still one of the most famous speeches in American history.

Gettysburg wasn't the bloodiest or the longest battle, but it did mark the beginning of the end of the Civil War. When the smoke cleared, the North had won a **critical** victory. The tide had turned. Although the war continued for nearly 2 more years, General Robert E. Lee never again won a major battle. We remember Gettysburg for Lincoln's famous address, and also because it was the beginning of the end of the Civil War.

resolve: promise   **in vain**: without good reason   **perish**: disappear from   **critical** (**krit** uh kuhl): important

51

Lucius remained in Gettysburg only a few days. His arm was buried in a tin box in the garden of the house where he had **recuperated**. Lucius did not complain about the pain or about the loss of his arm, but he did grieve the loss of his men. He learned that of the 273 men that had arrived at Gettysburg under his command, only 40 were still able to fight.

Lucius returned to Wisconsin to heal and to think about his future and the future of the men who had survived, as well as the future of the families of the men who had died fighting.

HARPERS WEEKLY 8/08/63

The Battle of Gettysburg was a turning point in the Civil War in favor of the Union forces.

recuperated (re **koo** puh ray tid): gotten better after an injury or illness

7

The Hero as Governor

Lucius's sister and mother cared for him as he recovered in his home in Madison. He called his house "Headquarters, One-Armed Corps."

The **stump** was healing well, but he still felt pain where his arm should have been, as if it were still there. Lucius heard a popular belief of the time. Some people felt that the part of the arm that was amputated and buried might be cramped, or crooked, causing pain. Lucius sent to Gettysburg for his buried arm. Shortly after receiving it, he felt that the pain gradually grew less **intense**.

---

stump: what is left after the main part is removed   **intense**: strong

Another Amputation

War causes a lot of pain and injury. It's not just that soldiers die. Many are wounded in ways that affect them the rest of their lives. This story comes from a Union soldier named Private Lewis. The story of his amputation was published in the *Madison Democrat* newspaper, just as he reported it:

It was the second battle of Bull Run, which was August 28, and 29, 1862. During the second fight, while we were crossing a stone wall, I [Private Lewis] was shot through the left arm just below the elbow. Nevertheless, I marched twelve miles that day in spite of my wound. The next day my arm was found to be so badly shattered that amputation below the elbow was necessary. The operation was performed without **chloroform** [or] (**anesthetic**), and the arm was buried on the battlefield. Then I was sent on to Washington to recuperate in the hospital there.... I didn't heal as rapidly as I should have as the bone in my arm had been shattered and after a time, **gangrene** set in. It was found that in order to save my life a second operation was necessary, and so I had a second operation of the same arm, this time near the shoulder. The amputated arm was sent by the surgeons to the army museum in that city, where for years it was displayed in a bottle in a case.... The arm had given me trouble

chloroform (**klor** uh form): a liquid once given to patients before surgery; after they breathed it in, they felt much less pain   anesthetic (an uhs **thet** ik): a substance that causes a lack of feeling as well as sleepiness
gangrene (**gan** green): death and decay of part of the body

for a long time, and some time ago while my daughter was going to the museum she came upon the arm, and remembering her father's complaints and the **superstitions** concerning amputated members she asked that the arm be laid on its side instead of standing on end in the bottle. The museum complied with her request. Later on, when the arm was giving me less trouble, she told me what she had done. I laughed and said I took no stock in such superstitions, but she laughed also and reminded me that my arm had not been troubling me of late.

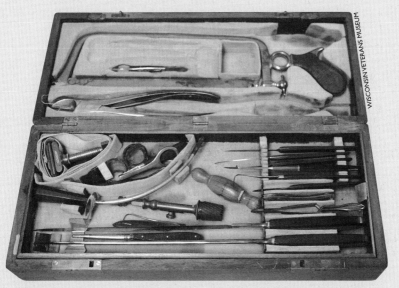

WISCONSIN VETERANS MUSEUM

The Civil War was a very bloody war, and amputations were common. This amputating kit belonged to Dr. Erastus Buck, from Marquette, Wisconsin.

superstition (soo per **stish** uhn): a belief that is based on fear or hope

The Wisconsin Republican Party held its convention later that summer. The state's Republicans had Lucius run for Wisconsin secretary of state. Though he had been a Democrat before the war, he now felt closer to the beliefs of the Republican Party. He accepted the **nomination**.

Lucius's father had taught Lucius that the best politicians are those who don't appear to want to be politicians. In his acceptance speech, he said, "I wish to **tender** you many thanks for the honor you have done me. . . . I have no political **aspirations**. I ask no office." Lucius adopted this approach through most of his political career.

The Republicans used the loss of his arm to **emphasize** his leadership and sacrifice in the war. In their speeches and **editorials**, phrases such as "an empty sleeve," "loss of the left arm," "Colonel Fairchild's wound," and "the field of Gettysburg," appeared over and over again. Lucius was a great hero, and his empty sleeve was a powerful reminder of his heroism and sacrifice.

---

nomination: being chosen to run in an election   **tender**: give   **aspirations** (as puh **ray** shuhnz): goals
emphasize: draw attention to   **editorial** (ed uh **tor** ee uhl): an article in a newspaper or magazine where the writer gives his or her opinion on something

Lucius spoke about patriotism in his speeches, and he worked for the support of soldiers. He wanted to be seen as "the soldiers' choice" in this election.

Lucius was a colonel, and he was proud of his place in the army. However, a month before the election, the Democrats **stunned** him by **revealing** that Wisconsin's state constitution said that a man could not hold office and be in the army at the same time. Lucius would have to choose which he wanted more. He wasn't sure what he should do.

He went to Washington to talk with a family friend, who advised him to **resign** from the army. The friend understood that Lucius had been nominated for secretary of state, without seeking the office. He said, "You will be the next governor of our state," and he gave Lucius some political advice. "Do well the work in hand and your success is **assured**." Lucius must not "seem to look beyond the office of Secretary of State," and "when the Office of Governor is suggested to you—Know Nothing." The friend's advice to him was similar to that of Jarius Fairchild. The best political **strategy** was to remain modest.

stunned: shocked   **revealing**: making known   **resign**: give up a position or job   **assured**: guaranteed
strategy (strat uh jee): plan for achieving a specific goal

Many people at the time felt that public **ambition** would get in the way of success. Lucius would seem more popular if others wanted him for a job, rather than if he himself were pushing for it.

Lucius also met with Abraham Lincoln during this trip to Washington. Two days after the meeting, Lincoln wrote, "Let Colonel Lucius Fairchild of Wisconsin be appointed a **Brigadier General** of Volunteers." Lucius's political career received a great lift from this appointment. He was now a man who had entered the army as a captain and left as a top general. Between his rank and his wound, Lucius Fairchild made an ideal political candidate.

Lucius resigned his newly appointed role as general. However, he did keep the title, and from then on, he was often referred to as General Fairchild.

Lucius met with many Wisconsin soldiers while in Washington as well. He hoped that they would support his bid for election. The election was held one week later, in November of 1863. With the help and the influence of

ambition: strong desire to succeed   **brigadier general**: a high-ranking military officer, ranking above a colonel

"the boys in blue," as the Union soldiers were known, Lucius Fairchild was elected Wisconsin's secretary of state.

Lucius Fairchild worked 10 to 12 hours a day at his new job. He made sure that the money that the state received was well accounted for and that taxes were fair.

A large part of his work also involved helping returning soldiers to find work and get the medical care they needed.

Lucius had a genuine concern for veterans' families. He helped families receive health care and pay when their men were away in the war. He also knew that every time he helped someone, he helped the Republican Party as well.

At this time, Lucius began his own family. In April of 1864, he married Frances Bull, who was more commonly called "Frank." She was from Detroit, Michigan, and Lucius had met her in Washington during the war. According to all accounts, Frank was **stately** and charming. She had dark hair and dark eyes. She was quick to laugh but still very **dignified**. Lucius loved her very much, and she made the perfect wife for a

stately: graceful   **dignified**: appearing like a lady or gentleman

politician on the rise. In time, they had three daughters—Mary, Sally, and Caryl.

When Wisconsin's governor James T. Lewis said that he would not seek another term, Lucius was ready to be the next governor. But he did not make such an announcement. Instead, he encouraged his old military friends to put his name forward. They wrote letters to the newspapers, **urging** that Lucius should be the next governor. Lucius was then able to point out to others that

WHI IMAGE ID73448

Governor Lucius Fairchild with his wife, Frances, in Madison.

urging: recommending strongly

"the soldiers seem determined that I shall be Governor," as he showed the clippings from the paper.

Once he had the support of the soldiers, he worked to get support from **civilians** and from the newspapers. He always appeared to be reasonably **humble** and ready to serve—a simple soldier doing the will of the people.

For example, many in the Republican Party wanted African Americans to be able to vote, but the official party **policy** was against it. Although Lucius thought that blacks should be allowed to vote, he did not say so publicly. He didn't want to stir up too much **controversy**. He did not let his personal views on the matter **dominate** what he thought was best politically.

When he was formally nominated for governor, he said, "the office must seek the man." Although Lucius really wanted the office, he had managed to make it appear as if he were merely agreeing to what others wanted of him. In November of 1865, Lucius Fairchild was elected governor by a **landslide victory**.

civilian (suh **vil** yuhn): someone who is not in the armed forces   **humble**: not proud   **policy** (**pol** uh see): plan of action   **controversy** (**kon** truh vur see): dispute or argument   **dominate**: control   **landslide victory**: an election won by a great many votes

Lucius began his first term by attacking those who supported the South. The war was over, but bad feeling and conflict continued. Some people wanted to punish the South for starting the war. Others wanted to move toward forgiveness.

Lucius was among those who wanted to punish the South. He had been deeply affected by the loss of his men in the war, and he found that he could not forgive the South for leaving the Union.

In his first speech as governor, he praised those who had fought in the war. "When there was **mourning** in so many of our homes . . . still mothers sent forth other sons . . . our country's calls were answered . . . thousands have fallen in the conflict. . . . They have saved this nation."

Within 6 months of being elected, Fairchild issued a **proclamation** giving African Americans the right to vote. He also encouraged immigrants from other countries to come to Wisconsin.

---

mourning: feeling sadness or grief for someone who has died   **proclamation** (prok luh **may** shuhn): an official announcement

For much of his first term, Fairchild gave his attention to national questions about how to deal with freed slaves and the Southern states. At the time, a governor's term lasted only 2 years. It was soon time for him to run again.

His campaign again emphasized his military service. Newspapers used phrases such as "the empty sleeve" and "the heroic commander of the Old Wisconsin Second." Lucius continued to depend on his reputation as a former military leader to win the support of veterans. In November 1867, he won election to a second term.

Lucius celebrates the Fourth of July with family and friends in 1893.

In his second term, Lucius Fairchild worked in 3 major areas. First, he supported more money for education. He urged schools to adopt modern teaching methods and to raise teachers' salaries.

Second, he helped children who had been made **orphans** by the war. In Madison, he supported Cordelia Harvey, who had been a Civil War nurse. She **converted** a soldiers' hospital into an orphanage for soldiers' surviving children. In fact, Lucius used to take children for boat rides on Lake Monona and for picnics on Sundays.

Third, Lucius worked to improve transportation. He wanted to see a canal built that would link the Wisconsin and Fox rivers, so that goods could move between the Great Lakes and the Mississippi River by water. He also worked for fair rates for railroad transportation, so that farmers could make a decent living when they sent their goods to market.

His wife, Frank, helped him a great deal in his job as governor. She was a **gracious hostess**. One writer described her as "a woman of great beauty, charm." Another writer at the

orphan (or fuhn): a child whose parents are dead   **converted**: changed into a different form
gracious hostess (gray shuhs hoh stis): a woman who makes guests feel comfortable

time said, "During this time Mrs. Fairchild helped her husband as few women could. . . . She always welcomed her husband's friends and with her **tact** and charm made the shyest **legislator** feel at home."

When Lucius had only one year left in his second term, he was thinking about his own political future. He wanted to become a U.S. **senator** from Wisconsin, but the Republican Party chose a different candidate. Lucius needed a job to pay family bills. Being governor had paid well, but he had debts and businesses that needed cash.

Lucius Fairchild decided to run for a third term as governor, even though no one else before him had ever served 3 terms. He had many advantages. He was known for honesty and clean government. He was still seen as a war hero. And he had traveled around the state, listening to people to try to understand how state government could help them improve their lives.

tact: the ability to say and do the right thing   **legislator** (**lej** is lay tur): lawmaker   **senator**: a person elected to serve in the Senate, one of the 2 bodies of the branch of government that makes laws

However, as he had before, Lucius hid his own ambition. He made it seem as if he were running only because he had been asked to.

He gave many campaign speeches as he traveled around Wisconsin. Lucius didn't see himself as a great speaker, but he was convincing. He said, "I don't think I am much of a speaker. The only thing which comforts me . . . is that I never had an audience leave till I had finished."

In 1869, he was re-elected governor. He was determined to **justify** the people's faith in him.

He remained a very popular leader. The *Milwaukee Daily Sentinel* called him a "capable and efficient governor, and the most popular one that the state has ever had."

In the autumn of 1871, Lucius was preparing for his final months in office. It should have been a quiet time for him.

However, on October 8, the Chicago Fire began to burn out of control. Much of the city burned to the ground.

justify (**jus** tuh fi): give good reason for

Hundreds of people were killed. As soon as Lucius heard about the **tragedy**, Lucius hurried south to Illinois to offer his help. However, he had barely arrived there when he learned that an even larger fire had destroyed much of northeastern Wisconsin and killed many people.

The **Peshtigo** Fire started the same day as the Chicago Fire. It is still the largest recorded forest fire in North America.

The Peshtigo Fire swept through northeast Wisconsin in 1871. Frances acted quickly to provide relief to victims.

The weather had been very dry and hot. Dry trees and dry **slash** in this lumber country were ready to burn. The conditions were perfect for a forest fire.

tragedy (**traj** uh dee): a very sad event   Peshtigo (**pesh** ti goh)   **slash**: the branches and parts of trees too small to saw during logging

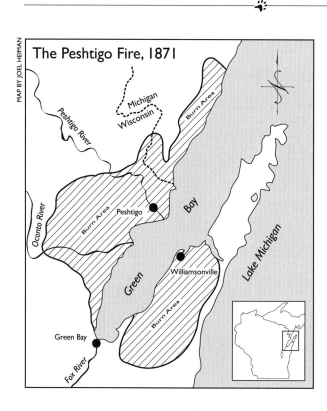

The Peshtigo Fire, 1871

MAP BY JOEL HEIMAN

No one knows exactly how the fire began. An unusual wind swept flames across the crowns of the tall pines in the northern forests. The village of Peshtigo itself was destroyed in minutes. The fire burned well over 1 million acres, an area twice the size of Rhode Island. The fire was so hot that it created a "fire tornado" with circling winds strong enough to fling houses and railroad cars into the air. The heat was so intense that the flames actually jumped miles across the waters of Green Bay and started fires in Door County. There it destroyed the community of Williamsonville!

The fire reduced 12 towns to ashes, and millions of trees were lost. It killed more than 1,000 people. Thousands more were left injured and homeless.

Lucius returned immediately from Chicago to Madison. His wife had already started to provide help. The book, *Wisconsin Pioneer Women*, describes Frances's efforts for the victims of the fire:

> While Mrs. Fairchild never desired power for herself, there was one time when she had on her own **initiative** to act as Governor of Wisconsin. It was during the Chicago fire when the governor and all the state officers were in Chicago in conference to see what could be done to help. The women of Madison were gathering clothes and supplies to send down to the fire victims as soon as the orders should arrive at the city hall. Late one night word came in from Peshtigo in northern Wisconsin that part of the State was all on fire, and would the governor please send help. Such a message could not be ignored and so, as there was no officer in town to **authorize** a plan, Mrs. Fairchild gave the orders herself. Knowing that the entire

initiative (I **nish** uh tiv): deciding what to do without being told by someone else   **authorize** (aw thur Iz): give permission to

country was rushing to the aid of Chicago, she gathered the clothes and supplies from the City Hall and ordering a special train, sent them to the little northern town where they were so much needed. The act was **characteristic** of her; to see what to do and to do it, but never to seek any power ... for herself.

Lucius took nearly $10,000 from the state's general fund to use for fire victim relief. Then he hurried to Green Bay, the largest city in the burned-over area. Dealing with this emergency required him to move quickly and effectively. He knew how to deal with **crisis** from his days in the army.

Relief committees had been slow to get started, but Lucius energized them into working efficiently and carefully. He was determined that everyone who had suffered from the fire should receive housing, food, and a way to make a living, as quickly as possible.

Committees in Marinette, Green Bay, Milwaukee, and Sturgeon Bay helped thousands of people whose property had been destroyed. The winter was approaching, and people

characteristic (ker ick tuh **ris** tik): acting in a typical or usual way   **crisis** (**kri** sis): a time of danger or difficulty, or a turning point

had immediate needs for food, clothing, and shelter. But Governor Fairchild knew that people would also need help to rebuild their lives and communities.

He was chosen president of the Society for the Relief of the Sufferers by Fire in Northeast Wisconsin. He oversaw the collection of **donations** and also made sure that accurate records of expenses were kept. The desire to help others drove him. Throughout his many years of public life, he had always paid attention to those in need. His response to the Peshtigo Fire showed again how much he cared about Wisconsin's citizens.

During the days he ran the relief efforts. In the evenings he attended to normal state business. Lucius was so busy with attending to the fire's victims that he forgot about the upcoming elections and the help he had promised to give his party.

Although he was not running for office, many citizens wanted him to **reconsider**. His response to the fire had

donation: a gift of money or help   **reconsider**: to think about again shown them how effective his leadership was. One person wrote of him, "The **Universal** cry now is 'God Bless Governor Fairchild.'"

But Lucius did not change his mind. "I am to **retire** from public life," he replied. By December, he was cleaning out his office.

---

universal: of or belonging to everyone   **retire**: give up an office or occupation

8

Overseas and Back Again

Lucius had campaigned for Ulysses Grant when Grant ran for president in 1872. After Grant won, Lucius wanted a **diplomatic post**. So he **lobbied** to get President Grant to appoint him. Grant repaid Lucius by asking him to be **consul** to Liverpool, England.

Diplomats serve their country by working in foreign countries as representatives of their government. Diplomats help tourists and businesses that operate in both countries. They may also help in a political crisis, such as trying to avoid war or other kinds of conflicts. Diplomatic posts are often given to supporters as rewards for political help.

Lucius was ready. For more than 10 years he had worked in Wisconsin. He had governed effectively and pushed the Republican Party's interests in campaigns and lawmaking.

diplomatic post: a position where someone works to handle relations between his or her country and another country   **lobbied**: tried to influence someone to do something, especially in politics   **consul**: a government official living in a foreign country

He was tired. Although he was only 40 years old, many called him "the Old Man in Wisconsin." Lucius already had grey hair, and his face was **drawn** because he suffered from constant pain in the stump of his arm. He wanted more time with his family, and his new job would provide him with steady income and a rest from the demands of politics.

In late November of 1872, Lucius Fairchild and his family set sail for Liverpool, England. He made a comfortable living in England, and he was well respected, too. The work suited Lucius. He worked well with people, believed in helping, and was very familiar with how government worked.

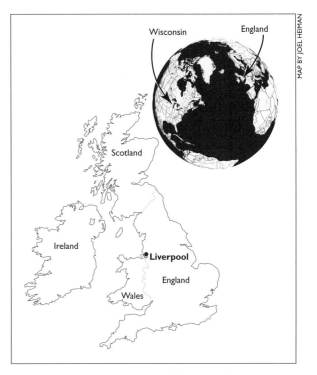

Lucius served as consul at Liverpool, England, from 1872 to 1878.

drawn: showing effects of pain or tension

One English newspaper reported, "There is no person living who has the same **mastery** over practical **principles** and details of **international** commerce."

After a few years, though, he wanted to return home to Madison. He felt old, although he was only 44. He said, "I am as grey as a grey horse, and my whiskers are nearly white." However, in 1878, he was appointed to be the consul in Paris, and one year later, Lucius was appointed to a diplomatic post in Spain. At last, in 1882, he was relieved of his post in Spain so that he could return home.

On the day Lucius arrived in Madison, he was met at the railroad station by a brass band and thousands of people, including political leaders. Madison's greatest hero had returned. Parents held up their children so that they could see, and people waved handkerchiefs and shouted. One Milwaukee veteran sent this greeting: "Every soldier's heart today beats a happy, hearty song of welcome to the loved one-armed patriot."

mastery: very great skill or knowledge   **principle**: a basic law or truth   **international**: relating to 2 or more nations

As he stood on a platform at the capitol, Lucius began to speak. "My heart is too full," he said. "It comes to but few men in the world to know the pleasure of returning home." Tears began to fill his eyes. "I can control myself no longer to talk to you," he said, and he turned away, looking back once to wave. The crowd went wild with shouting and loud applause.

His next few days were filled with visits and welcomes. As people greeted him, they also wondered about his political plans. He wrote to his wife, "Already I am nominated for President by several papers—much to my **disgust** . . . all I want is to be let alone politically." However, many of his friends did not believe that he meant what he said. They continued to ask about politics. Lucius wrote his wife, "If a fellow can judge by the papers your old husband is very much of a candidate. Let us see, the list is about as follows: President—Vice President—Senator—Congressman—Minister to England—and perhaps **Alderman** of Madison. . . . Well, we will surprise them by not having anything."

Lucius changed his mind, though. He finally did announce that he would be willing to serve as senator.

disgust: a strong feeling of dislike   **alderman**: representative

It was a mistake. Although he had much popular support, many politicians in Wisconsin wanted a different candidate. Lucius was defeated in the election and was bitterly disappointed. He decided he would never again run for office.

Instead, Lucius turned his attention to veterans groups. He was very active as a speaker and leader, and Wisconsin veterans worked toward his election as commander in chief of the Grand Army of the Republic, or G.A.R., in 1886. The G.A.R. was a veterans organization, with membership open only to soldiers who had fought in the Civil War. In 1890, at its largest, the G.A.R. had nearly half a million members. The organization worked to help veterans with health and other problems. It eventually led to the creation of the Veterans Administration or VA. The G.A.R. lasted until 1956, when its last member died.

Soon after he was elected, Lucius began a tour of G.A.R. organizations. An earthquake had devastated Charleston, South Carolina. Even though Charleston was in the heart of the former Confederacy, Lucius hurried there to help.

Lucius had come a long way in his views of the South. He now spoke of forgiveness. When he talked to the Confederate veterans in Charleston, he said, "I have no bitter **animosities** and I know today if I should meet the soldier whose aim made this armless sleeve, I would grasp his hand by

WHI IMAGE ID 73453

Lucius and the men with him were all G.A.R. members.

the only hand he left me and have no hard feelings toward him."

animosity (an uh **mos** uh tee): hatred

9

Lucius's Legacy

When Lucius's term as commander in chief was over, the G.A.R. showed their appreciation for their outgoing leader by arranging to have his portrait painted by John Singer Sargent, the most successful **portrait painter** of his **era**. Sargent was also a gifted landscape painter and watercolorist.

Lucius sat for hours for the artist. He wrote to his wife, "Mr. Sargent has been here all the morning but certain windows had to be changed so that a proper light can be shed on the manly form and **amiable** face of your husband.... He told me he will want some ten days."

Afterward, Lucius looked at the finished portrait and reported that it looked like "a lot of **badges** running off with a bald-headed man."

portrait painter: an artist who paints pictures of people   **era**: a period of time in history
amiable (**ay** mee uh buhl): friendly   **badge**: a ribbon or medal given for outstanding performance, often worn on a jacket

79

Lucius spent the last years of his life campaigning for Republican candidates, attending to his business interests, and enjoying his family. He strongly supported the University of Wisconsin, because he recognized the value of education for the state's citizens.

Lucius was also very interested in history. He frequently gave talks about the Civil War to veterans and civic groups. He was on the board

This portrait of Lucius was painted by John Singer Sargent in 1880. Sargent was one of America's leading portrait painters at the time.

of the State Historical Society of Wisconsin, and one person wrote that "To Lucius Fairchild, perhaps more than any other person, was **due passage** of the **act** providing for the noble building [of the Wisconsin Historical Society], which will in some sense be his **monument**."

due passage: passed because of   **act**: law   **monument** (**mon** yuh muhnt): something set up to honor the memory of a person or event

WHI IMAGE ID 44754

Lucius was a strong supporter of the Wisconsin Historical Society. This is how the Wisconsin Historical Society building looked in 1900, when it was built. You can still visit it today.

Lucius spent time with his family. He also spent some time taking care of his business interests. But he did not live much longer. On May 23, 1896, he died of severe flu and kidney failure at the age of 64.

Lucius was remembered kindly. Charles Adams, president of the University of Wisconsin, said, "He had an open and kind heart that went out to the poor as well as to the rich. His kindly feeling was as universal as his **charity** and his **generosity**."

charity (**char** uh tee): the act of giving to people in need   **generosity** (jen uh **ros** uh tee): willingness to share what you have

81

Lucius Fairchild had lived a full life. He had been a prospector, businessman, soldier, governor, diplomat, and community supporter. His heroism gave him the opportunity to serve his state and his country, and he responded unselfishly and honestly.

True heroes use their fame and reputation to help others, as he did. It is that service to the people of Wisconsin that makes us remember Lucius today. His empty sleeve came to symbolize his bravery, sacrifice, and commitment to the state and the country he loved.

WHI IMAGE ID 2324 7

Lucius was honored as both a governor and Civil War hero during his funeral in 1896.

Appendix

Lucius's Time Line

1831 — Lucius Fairchild is born in Portage County, Ohio, on December 27.

1846 — Lucius's family moves to Madison.

1849 — Lucius goes to California in search of gold.

1855 — Lucius returns to Madison.

1858 — Lucius is elected clerk of Dane County court.

1861 — Lucius volunteers to join the Union army.

1863 — Lucius loses his arm at the Battle of Gettysburg on July 1.

Lucius is elected Wisconsin's secretary of state in November.

1864 — Lucius marries Frances Bull in April.

1865 — Lucius is elected governor of Wisconsin.

1867 — Lucius wins re-election as governor

1869 — Lucius is elected governor for a third term.

1872 — President Grant appoints Lucius consul at Liverpool, England.

1878 — Lucius is appointed consul-general at Paris.

1880 — Lucius is appointed U.S. minister to Spain

1886 — Lucius is elected commander in chief of the G.A.R.

1896 — Lucius dies in Madison on May 23.

Glossary

Pronunciation Key

a   c<u>a</u>t (kat), pl<u>ai</u>d (plad),
     h<u>al</u>f (haf)

ah f<u>a</u>ther (**fah** <small>TH</small>ur),
     h<u>ea</u>rt (hahrt)

air c<u>a</u>rry (**kair** ee), b<u>ea</u>r (bair),
     wh<u>ere</u> (whair)

aw <u>a</u>ll (awl), l<u>aw</u> (law),
     b<u>ou</u>ght (bawt)

ay s<u>ay</u> (say), br<u>ea</u>k (brayk),
     v<u>ei</u>n (vayn)

e   b<u>e</u>t (bet), s<u>ay</u>s (sez),
     d<u>ea</u>f (def)

ee b<u>ee</u> (bee), t<u>ea</u>m (teem),
     f<u>ea</u>r (feer)

i   b<u>i</u>t (bit), w<u>o</u>men (**wim** uhn),
     b<u>ui</u>ld (bild)

ı   <u>i</u>ce (ıs), l<u>ie</u> (lı), sk<u>y</u> (skı)

o   h<u>o</u>t (hot), w<u>a</u>tch (wotch)

oh <u>o</u>pen (**oh** puhn), s<u>ew</u> (soh)

oi b<u>oi</u>l (boil), b<u>oy</u> (boi)

oo p<u>oo</u>l (pool), m<u>o</u>ve (moov),
     sh<u>oe</u> (shoo)

or <u>or</u>der (**or** dur), m<u>ore</u> (mor)

ou h<u>ou</u>se (hous), n<u>ow</u> (nou)

u   g<u>oo</u>d (gud), sh<u>ou</u>ld (shud)

uh c<u>u</u>p (kuhp), fl<u>oo</u>d (fluhd),
     butt<u>o</u>n (**buht** uhn)

ur b<u>ur</u>n (burn), p<u>ea</u>rl (purl),
     b<u>ir</u>d (burd)

yoo <u>u</u>se (yooz), f<u>ew</u> (fyoo),
     v<u>iew</u> (vyoo)

hw <u>wh</u>at (hwuht), <u>wh</u>en (hwen)

<small>TH</small> <u>th</u>at (<small>TH</small>at), brea<u>the</u> (bree<small>TH</small>)

zh mea<u>s</u>ure (**mezh** ur),
     gara<u>ge</u> (guh **razh**)

act: law

alderman: representative

ambition: strong desire to succeed

ambushed: attacked from a hiding place

amiable (**ay** mee uh buhl): friendly

amputate (**am** pyuh tate): cut off all or part of a finger, arm, or leg because of disease or injury

anesthetic (an uhs **thet** ik): a substance that causes a lack of feeling as well as sleepiness

animosity (an uh **mos** uh tee): hatred

aspirations (as puh **ray** shuhnz): goals

assured: guaranteed

auction agent: person in charge of a public sale, where items are sold to the person offering the most money for them

authorize (**aw** thur Iz): give permission to

badge: a ribbon or medal given for outstanding performance, often worn on a jacket

bankrupt: without enough money to pay what a person owes

bayonet (bay uh **net**): a blade that can be attached to the front end of a rifle

benefit: anything that is for the good of someone or something

block and tackle: a device with a heavy weight at one end, a pulley in the middle, and a hook on the other end; it makes the task of lifting heavy objects easier

brigadier general: a high-ranking military officer, ranking above a colonel

casualty (**kazh** oo uhl tee): someone who has been wounded, killed, or injured in a battle

ceremonial (ser uh **moh** nee uhl): taking place for a traditional or formal purpose more than for practical use

characteristic (ker ick tuh **ris** tik): acting in a typical or usual way

charity (**char** uh tee): the act of giving to people in need

chloroform (**klor** uh form): a liquid once given to patients before surgery; after they breathed it in, they felt much less pain

civilian (suh **vil** yuhn): someone who is not in the armed forces

clatter: an attempt or a try

clerk: someone who works in an office and files records

commerce: the buying and selling of goods in large amounts

communication (kuh myoo nuh **kay** shun): giving and receiving information

competent (**kom** puh tuhnt): capable

conceived: thought of or imagined

Confederate (kuhn **fed** ur it): relating to the 11 Southern states that fought the Northern states in the American Civil War

confirmed: approved of

consecrate: to make sacred

consul: a government official living in a foreign country

controversy (**kon** truh vur see): dispute or argument

87

conveniently (kuhn **vee** nyuhnt lee): easily

convention: a large gathering of people from the same political party

converted: changed into a different form

crisis (**krI** sis): a time of danger or difficulty, or a turning point

critical (**krit** uh kuhl): important

customs official: a person who collects taxes, paid to the government, on items brought in from foreign countries

debt (det): money that is owed to someone

dedicated: committed

delegate (**del** uh git): someone who is given power or authority to act for others

Democratic Party: one of the 2 main political parties in the United States

deprived: kept from

detract: take away from

devotion: a strong feeling of loyalty

dignified: appearing like a lady or a gentleman

diplomatic post: a position where someone works to handle relations between his or her country and another country

discharged: carried out; performed

disgust: a strong feeling of dislike

dominate: control

donation: a gift of money or help

draft: the selection of people for a special purpose, especially for serving in the army

drawn: showing effects of pain or tension

drill: lesson on how to do something by doing it over and over again

dry goods store: a general store selling a variety of items, such as sugar, tools, and cloth

due passage: passed because of

editorial (ed uh **tor** ee uhl): an article in a newspaper or magazine where the writer gives his or her opinion on something

emphasize: draw attention to

encounter: an unexpected meeting or conflict

endeavored (en **dev** urd): tried

endure: keep on

entitled (en **tI** tuhld): has a claim to

environment (en **vI** ruhn muhnt): the natural world of land, sea, and air in which people, animals, and plants live

era: a period of time in history

expanding: growing larger

expelled: forced to leave

expense: the money spent on something

fee: money paid for a service that is performed

financial (fI **nan** shuhl): having to do with money

formal: organized with a set of rules

formation: a special arrangement of troops and of military equipment

fortune: a great deal of money or property

4 score and 7 years: 87 years; a score is a group of 20

gallant (**gal** uhnt): brave

gangrene (**gan** green): death and decay of part of the body

generosity (jen uh **ros** uh tee): willingness to share what you have

glory: great praise and honor

governor: the person elected as the head of the state to represent all of the people of the state

gracious hostess (**gray** shuhs **hoh** stis): a woman who makes guests feel comfortable

grieved: felt sad for

habitat: the place or environment where a plant or animal naturally or normally lives

hallow: to make holy

heroism (**her** oh iz uhm): bravery

humble: not proud

immigrant (**im** uh gruhnt): a person from one country who moves to settle permanently in another

in vain: without good reason

initial (i **nish** uhl): first

initiative (i **nish** uh tiv): deciding what to do without being told by someone else

insecure: not confident of oneself

intense: strong

international: relating to 2 or more nations

invading: entering by force

investment: something purchased with the hope that it will generate additional money

invincible (in **vin** suh buhl): not able to be defeated

issue: a point to be debated

item: thing or object

justify (**jus** tuh fI): give good reason for

landslide victory: an election won by a great many votes

legislator (**lej** is lay tur): lawmaker

lieutenant (loo **ten** uhnt): a military rank below captain and above sergeant

limitation: where something ends

lobbied: tried to influence someone to do something, especially in politics

mangled: badly cut or torn

mastery: very great skill or knowledge

militia (muh **lish** uh): a volunteer army trained to fight only in an emergency

modest: not thinking too highly of oneself

monotonous (muh **not** uh nuhs): boring because of sameness

monument (**mon** yuh muhnt): something set up to honor the memory of a person or event

mourning: feeling sadness or grief for someone who has died

musket ball: a lead ball, similar to a bullet but larger, that is shot from a gun called a musket

nationally: across or throughout a nation

nerve: to work up the courage for

nomination: being chosen to run in an election

nugget: a small, rough piece of valuable metal

orphan (**or** fuhn): a child whose parents are dead

panning: washing gravel or sand in a pan, so the gold becomes separate

pass: a gap or place of lower elevation

perish: disappear from

policy (**pol** uh see): plan of action

political (puh **lit** uh kuhl): having to do with the way a city, county, state, or nation governs itself

politics: the way a city, state, or nation governs itself

polluting (puh **loot** ing): dirtying or destroying the natural environment

portion (**por** shuhn): a part

portrait painter: an artist who paints pictures of people

principle: a basic law or truth

proclamation (prok luh **may** shuhn): an official announcement

proposition: a plan or idea to be considered

prospector: someone who explores an area looking for valuable resources

provision (pruh **vizh** uhn): a supply of food

purchase: something that is bought

rebel: someone on the side of the Confederates in the Civil War

reconsider: to think about again

recruiting (re **kroo** ting): getting people to join a group, especially the military

recuperated (re **koo** puh ray tid): gotten better after an injury or illness

regiment (**rej** uh muhnt): part of the army (500 to 1,000 soldiers) under the command of a colonel

reputation (rep yoo **tay** shuhn): the opinion that people have about someone or something

resign: give up a position or job

resolve: promise

retire: give up an office or occupation

retreat: move back

revealing: making known

rill: a brook

rivulet: a very small stream

routine (roo **teen**): the regular or usual method for doing things

sacrifice (**sak** ruh fIs): the act of giving up one thing for another thing

salary (**sal** ur ee): money that you get paid for work that you do

secede (si **seed**): to leave or withdraw from a group or an organization, often to form another

senator: a person elected to serve in the Senate, one of the 2 bodies of the branch of government that makes laws

site: location, place

skirmish: a small battle

slash: the branches and parts of trees too small to saw during logging

slaughter: killing of many people

sombrero (som **brer** oh): a hat whose wide brim helps block the sun

staked claims: paid money for the chance to find gold in a specific location

stately: graceful

station: position

straightforward: honest, direct

strategy (**strat** uh jee): plan for achieving a specific goal

stump: what is left after the main part is removed

stunned: shocked

superstition (soo pur **stish** uhn): a belief that is based on fear or hope

surrendered (suh **ren** durd): given up

tact: the ability to say and do the right thing

tannery: a place where leather is made from animal hides

tax: money paid to the government

tender: give

territory (**ter** uh tor ree): land

tragedy (**traj** uh dee): a very sad event

treaty: an official written document between 2 nations

undisciplined (un **dis** uh plind): untrained or out of control

Union: the group of states that remained loyal to the United States government during the Civil War; the North

unity: (**yoo** ni tee): being in agreement

universal: of or belonging to everyone

upbringing: the care and training given to children when they are growing up

urging: recommending strongly

vegetation (vej uh **tay** shuhn): plant life such as trees and grasses

veteran: someone who has lots of experience doing something

volley: a shower of bullets

wagon train: many wagons traveling together as a group

western: of or from the west. Iron Brigade troops came from Wisconsin, Indiana, and Michigan—which were then considered western states.

yoke up: attach work animals to a wood frame, or yoke, so they can pull a wagon or other equipment

Reading Group Guide and Activities

Discussion Questions

- Lucius left home to be part of the gold rush, but in the end he made money not from gold but by selling goods to miners. If there were a gold rush today, what kinds of supplies would people need that would be the same? What would be different?

- Lucius was an ambitious man. What are your ambitions? Who else do you consider ambitious?

- During the Civil War, battles took place in fields and forests, and soldiers were always within close range of the other soldiers they fought. How were Civil War battles similar to wars today, and how were they different?

- Lucius did not want to put himself forward for political office. Instead he appeared to let others recruit him. How do most candidates in our times run for office?

- Lucius responded very quickly to the Peshtigo Fire. What natural disasters have happened in our lifetimes, and what has the government done?

- During the Civil War, Lucius spoke with hatred about the South. How do you think Lucius later came to forgive the South for its role in the war?

Activities

- Research meals typically eaten by pioneers on wagon trains, prospectors in gold rush towns, and soldiers in the Civil War. Cook a meal with items from one of these situations.

- Make your own map of a Civil War battle. Show where different groups of soldiers attacked and retreated.

- Write a letter to your family as if you were a prospector, a Civil War soldier, or a survivor of the Peshtigo Fire. Find real examples of such letters, and compare them to what you have imagined.

- Visit your local historical society or museum and draw or take pictures of items, such as medals, bullets, or cookware, from the Civil War.

- Interview your family to see if you can learn a story about a family member who set off on a journey to a faraway place in search of a better life.

- Interview your family to see if you can learn a story from someone who was involved in a war.

To Learn More about the Civil War

Chang, Ina. *A Separate Battle: Women and the Civil War*. New York: Puffin, 1996.

Herbert, Janis. *The Civil War for Kids: a History with 21 Activities*. Chicago: Chicago Review, 1999.

Malone, Bobbie, and Kori Oberle. *Wisconsin: Our State, Our Story*. Wisconsin Historical Society Press, 2008.

McPherson, James M. *Fields of Fury: the American Civil War*. New York: Atheneum for Young Readers, 2002.

Murphy, Jim. *The Boys' War: Confederate and Union Soldiers Talk about the Civil War*. New York: Clarion, 1990.

Pferdehirt, Julia. *Caroline Quarlls and the Underground Railroad*. Wisconsin Historical Society Press, 2008.

Stanchak, John E. *Eyewitness: Civil War*. New York: Dorling Kindersley, 2000.

Wroble, Lisa A. *Kids during the American Civil War*. New York: PowerKids, 1997.

Acknowledgments

A book's publication always feels like something of a victory. Like a battle campaign, creating a book requires many people in different roles to work together. I'm grateful for the help I received in writing the story of Lucius Fairchild.

The Wisconsin Historical Society Press staff is exceptional. Mallory Kirby researched images, and John Nondorf brought that research to life with high-resolution scans. Joel Heiman plotted the course of Lucius's story with maps, and Dawn Shoemaker copyedited the manuscript with care. Mike Nemer and Elizabeth Boone guided the overall production of the book. I am grateful for all of their work.

Bill Brewster of the Veterans Museum was generous with his time, with his expertise, and with images and artifacts for the book. His knowledge about the Civil War runs deep, and the story is much improved for his assistance.

John Motoviloff edited the final manuscript with a careful eye and a light touch.

Bobbie Malone was a gentle general, overseeing the book from the beginning, always reminding me about the core of Lucius's story and its importance to Wisconsin.

Special thanks to my friends, my family, and my wife, Heather, my darling from Darlington. Last of all, thanks to the thousands of teachers and children who have welcomed me into their schools to share songs, stories, and the pleasure of living in our great state of Wisconsin.

Index

This index points you to the pages where you can read about persons, places, and ideas. If you do not find the word you are looking for, try to think of another word that means about the same thing.

When you see a page number in **bold** it means there is a picture on that page.